The Evolution of FINANCE

"This is a remarkable volume, written quite eloquently and insightfully, which represents a head-turner perspective on some rather revolutionary content. Barbara Guth sets an exciting tone for the book, as she frames it by using a quotation from a poem by Ruby Altizer Roberts, where he shares the beauty of Walter Russell's wisdom. I feel in effect she begins by "*dipping her own pen, molding her imaginative ideas, tuning them to 21st century times, and nesting them in moral terms*". The author set his *"**Secrets of The Universe**" whereas her* "***Platform of Wisdom***" is an offering for a sustainable world of finance through her ***new vision."***

Importantly, she sets the tone for the entire book in her Preface by directly addressing some technical nuances and realities, monetary policies, financial frameworks, investment strategies and the whole construct of "Venture Capital" in the interdependent, international financial world. She presents a highly logical walk through of our choices over the last 100 years of finance, thus revealing their resulting implications. What the author does is to directly address the existing financial world that was essentially founded in the mid-1940's shortly after the 1944 Bretton Woods Conference in New Hampshire, "*The United Nations Monetary and Financial Conference*. The delegates to that conference came from 44 nations and collectively agreed upon a series of new rules for the post-WWII international monetary system, most often enabled and supported by law such as the Federal Reserve System in the US, the European Central Bank for 19 countries in the European Union, and by the Central Banks throughout the Asia-Pacific region.

From that beginning of an interconnected international world of finance, it is hard to not be moved by Barbara's spirit of innovation and her foundational ideas for a 21st world of finance and investments. She nests her ideas for a world of mutual respect and as she writes in the Preface and in her thoughts saying: *Love and Respect for creation and for all of life.* This is a perspective that has been sadly lost, forgotten, or ignored through the tides of time. We need to find it again.

This book represents a clear analysis, a new vision, and a proposal for the future, all placed in a very human context. This context is compelling as it serves all humanity and not just the world of finance or investments. It represents a remarkable treatise on the future of our financial and investment worlds and is a must-read. With my adaptation of her words, she concludes that we "*will need some new tools, we'll need to shift our ways of thinking to enable change and create hope, we will need new and different enabling priorities that create new, innovative tools that will create a 21st world of finance, and she concludes by asking us to install a sense of love and human understanding by daring to change, and by daring to use some old-fashioned audacity!*"

—DR. ROBERT W. CORELL,
GLOBAL SCIENCE FOR A SUSTAINABLE FUTURE,
"HE WAS RECOGNIZED WITH THE OTHER SCIENTISTS FOR THE 2007 NOBEL PEACE PRIZE FOR HIS WORK WITH AND IN THE FOUNDING OF THE INTERNATIONAL PANEL ON CLIMATE CHANGE (IPCC) ASSESSMENTS".

What I loved most about Barbara's insightful book "The Evolution of Finance" is that I could not put it down! I found it captivating, inspiring, thoughtful and provocative, and read it all in one sitting! Barbara beautifully assisted me, a visionary in the healthcare world with a long history in philanthropy, by firstly validating my concerns. Having less of a background in the financial world, she helped me to better understand the world of venture capital and the role it plays in funding, both positive and negative. I personally never liked how an inventor must sell out for some startup capital. I greatly appreciate Barbara's brilliant way of simplifying an assumed financial structure and turning it around to rely instead on the highest frequencies of Love, Trust and Integrity, three attributes that I value most, to protect and cultivate the creator, the entrepreneur, the sovereign one and my vision. I am in the process of creating INIC, an Institute for Neurological Integrative Care near Boston, which will be a premier world class neurological integrative care center of excellence, addressing all aspects of traumatic brain injury and other neurological conditions in ONE center. INIC's Center of Excellence is attracting a world-class multidisciplinary team of scientists, physicians, world renowned academic research institutes and medical centers, mental health experts, rehabilitation professionals and neuroscience specialists. Our center will be using frequencies that are changing healthcare, and therefore I am fascinated to have found a financial platform that is consciously based on these same high frequencies and values, reflected as sovereignty, trust and honor. With this approach, I can continue to dream and grow my center without having to give up my vision, or equity, unless I choose to on my own terms. Barbara's model affords the entrepreneur their continued sovereignty while raising aligned capital to fulfill their vision.

Barbara, thank you for giving me the honor to read your refreshing and riveting brainstorm for a new extraordinary platform.You are a systems buster and this model is tailor-made for those of us that share this quality!

—KRISTA DIRICO,
CEO, FOUNDER OF INIC,
INSTITUTE OF NEUROLOGICAL INTEGRATIVE CARE

"Barbara's writing is quite thought provoking in many ways. The idea of developing an alternative platform that provides protection for inventors and their interests is not only important but essential for optimizing innovative spirit. In a world in which the word "fair" seems to be thrown around rather arbitrarily, it's powerful and heartening to see someone putting effort into making company creation and advancement more equitable for those who were the initiators of an enterprise deemed attractive by investors and worthy of their hard-earned capital."

—TOM DUQUETTE,
MANAGING DIRECTOR,
MIRAKI INNOVATIONS

"I can't imagine how challenging it would be to think beyond the current world view, but I see that Barbara did it with a finesse that only a talented author and a researcher like herself could possibly do. She offers an unapologetically realistic delivery regarding how many entrepreneurs and innovative creators feel in relation to the current financial sector. If you dream about the possibility of a new business or the entrepreneurial world, I feel like this is an unflinchingly honest place to start. The hype around this book has admittedly made me eager to read it, and the its relevance and value is even more validated by the author's extensive experience meeting and engaging with people from different sectors in different parts of the world. It is a profound read, offering hope that a new world is possible should we recognize our innovators, their visions, and peacebuilders to help support them, in a new light. This author is one to read."

—DR. MUKTI SUVEDI,
PEACE AND INTERNATIONAL DEVELOPMENT
EXPERT PROFESSOR, EXECUTIVE COACH, MENTOR,
TRAINER, PEACEBUILDING, INTERNATIONAL
DEVELOPMENT, EMERGENCY RELIEF MANAGEMENT,
ENTREPRENEURSHIP

"Simplicity is the natural order of the universe which provides for all the eventual complexities we discover. It is the simplicity that also provides the stability to adapt to change over eons. Barbara shows us how to realign the "dog eat dog" entrepreneurial investment environment into a stable, resonating, and maintainable state through which simplicity and truth can become attainable again. This financial "inoculation" may very well protect our economy from cyclical failings."

—ROBERT J HENDERSON, M.D.,
FACS ORTHOPEDIC SPINE SURGEON,
DALLAS SPINE CARE

"In this cogent, well-articulated volume, Barbara Guth gives a succinct, clear-eyed picture of how venture capital structures not only stifle the innovation so sorely needed to address our global challenges but often exacerbates them. Her proposed alternative incentivizes mutual trust, creativity, and collaboration in domains that have been increasingly governed by greed and egoism. As an international peacebuilder, I have witnessed the power dynamics and financial systems that all too easily drive grievance, polarization, and violence. I have also experienced the human capacity to bridge the very deepest divides through structures that allow people to access their heartfelt hopes and ideals, recognize their interdependence, and work together for the common good. Ms. Guth offers a pathway to foster just this kind of transformational change."

—OLIVIA STOKES DREIER,
SENIOR PEACEBUILDING ADVISOR
AND FORMER EXECUTIVE DIRECTOR,
KARUNA CENTER FOR PEACEBUILDING

"Reading Barbara's book crystalized for me the importance of staying sovereign with my movie and television scripts. It's something I felt within but was unable to fully appreciate and articulate until now. It's reassuring to see someone has a plan for an alternative to current funding paradigms, and it's wonderful to have someone like Barbara championing the cause of creatives."

—CAPTAIN (RET) CHARLES (DALE) SYKORA,
FORMER SKIPPER OF THE USS DALLAS, UNMANNED
SYSTEMS EXPERT, EMERGING SCREEN
AND TELEPLAY WRITER

"I highly recommend this book. Ms. Guth clearly reveals with grace and understanding, the various ways that we have gone astray as a society in the financial industry. She helps us to realize that we have all participated in this together, and knowingly or not, we have created a situation that puts our wonderful country in danger. As she shows us a simple way to come back in from off the cliff to a place of stability, more security and a place that is more aligned with real value, it does relieve the heart. Together with clear heads and calm minds, we can co-create a new future with the wisdom shown in this book, and the hope that is throughout the words she has written."

—MICHELE COMBS,
NATIONAL ENERGY AND LEGISLATIVE CONSULTANT
FOUNDER AND PRESIDENT,
YOUNG CONSERVATIVES FOR ENERGY REFORM,
FORMER VP COMMUNICATIONS CHRISTIAN COALITION

"I'm blown away regarding the magnificent creation that Barbara's book potentially manifests. With the impending breakdown of so many sectors due to the misguided endeavors of big pharma, big government, big food factories and the meltdown of allopathic medicine, the ideas presented in this book are a welcome relief to any weary soul. Her new way of looking at things offers a real potential way out, and it does so with thoughtful insight. This book is a must read for everyone who has high hopes, and I admire her for her remarkable efforts to make this a better world for us all to live in."

—GUY OTIS DANIELSON III M.D.,
BOARD CERTIFIED NEUROSURGEON,
FOUNDER OF TEXAS SPINE & JOINT HOSPITAL,
AND FOUNDER OF INTEGRATIVE
HEALTH MATTERS IN TYLER, TX

"With the "The Evolution of Finance", Barbara Guth has produced a work of extraordinary elegance, simplicity, and relevance: one that will join the short list of works that are truly transformative. Challenging a paradigm is hard, especially if it is in a field which seems almost impervious to any questioning, let alone to change. Paradigms get dislodged only when we change our assumptions and beliefs about the way things are. Barbara challenges our Implicit beliefs not just about the world of finance, but of our relationship to the world, and to each other. This book creates a powerful alternative to the mechanistic and impersonal worldview that has dominated our policies, our governance system, and our financial structures for decades. Humankind is at a perilous juncture in its evolution, and we must radically dismantle the very foundations of the world of finance to invite in a sustainable alternative. Buckminster Fuller was prophetic when he said, "You never change things by fighting the existing reality. To change something, build a new model that makes the existing model obsolete." With this book, Barbara does precisely that."

—SUDHANSHU PALSULE-FELLOW,
CAMBRIDGE INSTITUTE FOR SUSTAINABILITY LEADERSHIP, UNIVERSITY OF CAMBRIDGE

"Our hope for sustainable peace in our world requires sound financial structures that inspire and evoke stability within and amongst nations. Barbara's proposal is a great innovation. For any leaders wanting to build a stable base for their societies, I highly recommend exploring the ideas in Barbara's book.".

—DR. JOSEPH SEBARENZI,
FORMER PRESIDENT OF THE RWANDAN PARLIAMENT

The Evolution of FINANCE

A New Vision *for* Entrepreneurial Innovation

BARBARA GUTH

www.SagesseSRTE.com
Design: Shapan Inc.
First Edition: April 2022

Distributed globally by Boss Media.
New York | Los Angeles | London | Sydney

Paperback ISBN: 978-1-63337-674-8
E-Book ISBN: 978-1-63337-675-5
LCCN: 2022917108

Printed in the United States of America
1 3 5 7 9 10 8 6 4 2

In honor of my Creator.

In dedication to the souls that left us
that September day in 2001.
This Is For You.

AWARENESS

Who dips his pen in golden flame of Truth,
Who molds a thing of beauty from dull clay,
Whose eyes are closed to all that seems uncouth,
Who tunes his life-notes to a silver lay....
Transcends all ills and hold no thought of death,
Nor feels a fear of grave or worm or clod,
But gives out Love with every moment's breath
And knows this truth, that he is one with God.

This poem is a dedication from Ruby Altizer Roberts for Walter Russell in the book written about Walter by Glenn Clark, entitled: *The Man Who Tapped The Secrets Of The Universe.*

CONTENTS

PREFACE

I HAVE WRITTEN THIS BOOK from a place of Love and Respect.

My Love and Respect for creation and for all of life. From my Love and Respect for the inventors who will be bringing us the new world through technologies which are designed to assist humanity as we move into our next highest expression of the "human collective."

I have also written this book as the fulfillment of a personal vow made within my own heart. I will not fail in my fulfillment of this vow. Therefore, this book and what it represents is deeply personal to me. The solution I am offering was birthed from a quiet fire ignited within me over 21 years ago, when I was compelled to begin diligently searching for answers to some of the largest, intractable problems that plague humanity.

I think I have found one of the common denominators.

Together, we shall see if it hits its mark.

INTRODUCTION

AS I MENTIONED IN THE PREFACE, I have been on a mission. I wanted to understand some things that were not interpreted from the media, not from the news and not from thought-leaders telling me how to think. I really wanted to see for myself.

As a result, I have been building global friendships and relationships during information-gathering trips around the world over the last 21 years, somewhat like a self-imposed, private due-diligence quest. I have found some very special hearts along the way. And some very special souls.

> I HAVE DONE ALL OF THIS WITH GREAT INTENTION AND CLEAR INTENT: TO SEE AND UNDERSTAND OUR CORE PROBLEMS AS CLEARLY AS POSSIBLE.

Secondly, I have been building my skill sets over the years to become more and more useful in a variety of ways. I knew inside that what I had at my disposal didn't cut it. I pray these trainings and teachings will bear their fruit in right timing, and in right order. Conflict transformation, international peace building, masters work in contemplative psychotherapy, a coaching certification, Satir work, mediation, spiritual teachings, energy work etc., etc. My friends and loved ones sometimes thought I was crazy doing all this, and I understand that. But something was driving me deep inside to keep going.

I can say that not all of it was necessarily enjoyable, but it has been highly informative and deeply revealing. In fact, I have found over the years that there has been an unanticipated side effect for me.

I have become more and more adept at freeing myself.

And I found that I really like Freedom.

But back to the main course.

What I have come to realize is that many of our intractable problems seem to be deeply intertwined with one very specific issue, and this one issue has greatly led us astray. It was manifested out of thin air just over 100 years ago, and it has become so insidious in all sectors, including in the finance industry, that we don't even see it anymore, let alone question it. The divergence generated by this scenario occurred gradually and quietly, yet its ramifications have rippled through time with significant and highly destructive implications for us all. It has impacted every sector, every aspect of human life, and frankly all life on this planet. I honestly had no inkling about any of this when I started my journey, and I most assuredly had no idea that I would end up where I am now, all these years later.

IGNITION

It all came to bear for me back in 2014 when I needed to resolve a particular challenge I encountered after having met a remarkably brilliant inventor. Following my years of research and relationship building, it was this particular meeting with this particular gentleman that became the actual trigger for creative action. He became the unexpected fulcrum in my life.

He was bringing something entirely new to the planet. It would affect every sector, and the economies of nation-states. He knew what he had in his hands. I had worked in the venture world for the last 20 years when I suddenly realized that I didn't have a full tool kit to address what he actually needed. Wait! What?! I was determined to help him, but I didn't know how. It took two years of deep reflection, imploring God to help me see what I was missing. Then suddenly the solution came in a vision that continually downloaded to me day and night over a four-to-five day period. Initially, I was shocked and a bit surprised that I had not seen it before, as I had been earnestly looking for a solution for almost two years! As I contemplated it all, clearly no one in over 100 years had seen it either, or they would have set it up already. If on the other hand they had indeed seen it, they clearly hadn't bothered to bring it into existence.

Regardless, as I pondered its implications more deeply over the following year, I came to understand that I needed to in fact reverse engineer this entire situation not just for him, but for all inventors and stakeholders. It was then that I began to realize that I had inadvertently addressed a core, underlying issue in the overall financial industry, which in turn revealed a hidden kernel of a rather nasty and intransigent problem.

It was through this organic process that this solution was conceived and born.

The solution I propose will impact every sector and every stakeholder. Not being naïve to the fact that I was entering the shark world of venture capital, private equity and high finance, the solution I brought needed to have some teeth. Real teeth in fact, that would demand appropriate respect or meaningful repercussions if none was given.

Indeed, I understood that for this to be an effective tool to enable a real shift in our trajectory, I needed to strengthen it. If I was going to later attempt to change actual policy by means of its successful introduction, it would be important to give it as many legs as possible.

My goal was to create a more formidable force of protection for those revolutionary inventors and visionaries who desire to stay sovereign and private. In fact, this solution enables all inventors, visionaries, or entrepreneurs to be able to retain their right to have FREE CHOICE, both for themselves, and for their companies.

This is a worthy endeavor in my estimation, and yet it is a perspective that is sorely lacking in the financial sector.

While the tool itself may look deceptively simple at first blush, its implications are not so. By creating a legally standardized, institutionalized tool that is inserted into the midst of the financial landscape coupled with the additional bang of blockchain, it could possibly represent an evolutionary leap in our financial structures should it become widely adopted. Why would that happen? Because it is logical. And because it fills an unmet need. And because it benefits every stakeholder including those with a voice and those without.

Behind it stands a strong vision and philosophy that may resonate with many who understand our financial systems are innately flawed, and our creators who long to be truly honored. We need core level change, yet we can also affect this change in as non-disruptive a manner as possible. In fact, this has been the challenge and my goal, and it has taken six years to bring this vision forward.

I must implore however, that more importantly than the tool itself is my desire to explain in greater depth the precursor which enabled this tool's conception.

THIS IS THE TRUE SECRET SAUCE AND THE KEY TO OUR WAY OUT.

The development of both the underlying vision and the deeper awareness which enabled this vision to reveal itself represents an important leap in consciousness. Grasping these keys will be powerful for many. These same keys that helped me specifically in the financial realm will help others transmute sectors in their realms of expertise as well. Systems must be deconstructed to a certain degree to allow change and new thinking to enter and transpire, so that a new direction can come forward.

This change in consciousness was personally reflected in me through a change first in my own priorities, which then eventually led to the creation of this solution. This shift rippled throughout my "system," just as a wave will ripple through a quiet pool following a thrown pebble. I later realized that while this happened within me, just one single individual, I could easily envision what could happen should others join in from their respective sectors. Critical mass to create a tsunami of change is not as hard to achieve as many might imagine. The key is that it must resonate, and innately so.

BUT WE NEED SOME NEW TOOLS,
AND WE DEARLY NEED A NEW MINDSET.

Consequently, I will be presenting the means to modify an aspect of the financial industry, our mindsets, and the implications for all stakeholders for doing so. I will specifically be sharing some insights I have regarding the journey of how we got to where we are now. I share this in the hopes that we may better understand how we collectively co-create our current reality in the business and financial sectors. In this way, perhaps we can become more refined in what we decide to co-create together through our own greater personal awareness, while also freeing ourselves from past choices.

By sharing and igniting this shift in consciousness in a very practical manner, we can enable true and lasting change, and the beauty is that we will have co-created this change together. Personally, I do admit that the idea of many of us re-empowering ourselves with new choices rather than being collectively victimized by the past choices of others is a rather satisfying thought.

So, I offer this book to inspire. I don't pretend to have all the answers, and I have only my own experiences to bring to the table. I hope others will join in with their insights. But together, I do believe we can endeavor to co-create a world that is better than the one we are currently experiencing. All we need is some hope, some different priorities, a new, standardized tool to make it fly and some daring, old-fashioned audacity!

Chapter 1

ENTER THE VC:

THE VENTURE CAPITAL MODEL

IT IS IMPORTANT TO UNDERSTAND right out of the gates that I am not anti-VC. In fact, I think they play an exceptionally important role in our economy while supporting significant innovation. I am simply unveiling some obvious flaws in the overall model itself, having taken the time to reflect upon all of this over the years. There are implications from our collective choice to use this model almost exclusively, which leads to inevitable outcomes in the context of a larger dynamic. I share these flaws with you, as well as my simple logic. I leave it up to you to decide if what I am saying makes sense.

IS VENTURE CAPITAL A TRUTH?

So, what if the VC model itself wasn't a "truth,"

but was simply some person's idea regarding the way we decided to fund new ventures? Who in fact made the decision that we had to do funding a certain way anyway? Or did the VC model organically evolve because it was so self-evident? Is there really and truly only one way to generally fund inventors or was it artificially set up that way, and subsequently given some legs to then act as a barrier to entry for other approaches? What do you think? Do you agree these may be some relevant questions to ask? Simple questions really, but they are important questions. Because frankly, in all the history of mankind, we have only been using this particular standardized VC approach to finance visionaries and inventors for the last 76 years or so. It's kind of a blip on the human timeline really, and the deeper question is, has it served us?

I remind you that all our current methodologies were merely something that someone thought up at one point in time to address an opportunity, a problem, or a challenge. Nothing is set in stone, unless of course we do in fact set it in stone.

Understand as well that I am not remotely implying any nefarious intent, as this solution could have initially been anyone's real and honest attempt to enable something to get done. Frankly, addressing that subject is not my interest.

MY INTEREST IS IN FIXING THINGS.

Hence time marches on, and time itself is the true revealer of the strengths and weaknesses of any idea. This is a natural evolutionary process, and it needs to occur. But rather than damning the whole concept when some parts of it don't work ideally in all cases, perhaps we could instead find a way to fine-tune or adapt it along the way to increase its effectiveness? Maybe we could add an entirely new tool or two into the picture, but from a different or more expanded perspective? What if we then found a way to enable them all to somehow work in concert together?

This is what I am aiming to do. Because there really is no need to throw the proverbial baby out with the bath water. Let's just change the bath water and get on with it.

UNDER THE MICROSCOPE WE GO.

Let's really examine this thing called the "VC" model. Once upon a time, someone decided to create the concept of "venture capital" as a means of supporting innovation and entrepreneurs.

It clearly serves humanity in many important ways, as it represents a trillion-dollar market sector, while also acting as a powerful economic engine in the economy. It has also proven its value by allowing and enabling some fantastic innovations to happen.

But in what instances does this model not work, and what are the implications of that? After all, it hasn't earned the reputation "vulture capital" for no reason. Sadly, the venture world is often referred to as a "rape and pillage" of so many inventors. I did not create these references, but they have surely been used over the years by many a disheartened inventor. I, myself have seen many good scenarios, but I have also witnessed the antithesis. Who does this venture model leave behind? Who is forced to use this model when they would prefer something else? Why are there no real or viable, institutionalized options out there for our inventors or our visionaries? Lastly and most importantly, what is the cost to us all because we have chosen to fund inventors this way, and then subsequently institutionalize this approach? What are the longer-term ramifications for society itself?

When someone initially set up these rules, they were most likely happenstance, as a simple means to enable some people to invest. Somewhere down the road though, some people decided this was the primary, almost exclusive way to do this, and it has come at the expense of the creator/inventor. Over time, it has become a cost to us all.

The investor is served, yes, but at what cost? What did we leave on the table? To achieve a return for the investor in the standard VC model, the primary options are to either sell of the company, merge their company with another, or take the company public. Regardless, the inventor generally needs to sell out their vision, their creations, and their sovereignty, all because they needed a little start-up money.

REALLY?

Beyond that, there are some serious issues to consider as we dive more deeply into the venture model.

Chapter 2

THE START UP DILEMMA

I CAN SHARE WITH YOU right out of the gates that there are a lot of inventors who don't want to sell their companies. There are also many inventors who do not want to go public. Many inventors and visionaries would honestly prefer to remain sovereign. However, free choice and free will are removed from the equation the moment an inventor engages with most VC arrangements. There can be some exceptions of course, but inherent in the model itself is a sellout. If that is your strategy as an inventor, that's fabulous and go for it, full speed ahead!

However, if it is not, your options are limited.

A HOLE IN THE INVESTMENT LANDSCAPE

Currently, the standard venture capital model offers a means of bringing a group of investors together into a fund to pool resources together for equity, to then share in an exit strategy, typically represented by an acquisition or an IPO (initial public offering).

What does not currently exist is a means for investors to pool resources in a broadly standardized manner that enables a different kind of participation over time. Again, pooling does occur from time to time.

> BUT THE EXISTENCE OF A TRILLION-DOLLAR VENTURE CAPITAL MARKET SECTOR, WITHOUT ITS MIRROR, I.E., A STANDARD MECHANISM ENABLING A "POOLED REVENUE SHARE" MARKET SECTOR IS GLARINGLY OBVIOUS.

It simply doesn't exist.

And yet this is a choice many inventors would appreciate having, as it enables them to retain their sovereignty. We have never explored this scenario before in any standardized manner. There are generally understood mechanisms within the financial industry that already exist to enable certain things to happen. However, there is nothing like what I have mentioned above.

Currently, the various ways to provide start-up funding or additional working capital to existing companies to enable a launch, nurture growth, an expansion or the introduction of new products are the following:

- venture capital
- private equity
- angel groups
- friends and family
- debt instruments
- hedge funds
- growth capital or mezzanine capital
- merchant banking
- SBA's (Small Business Administration Loans)
- institutional investors
- royalty funds
- incubators
- investment banks
- credit unions
- crowdfunding, etc.

Note that not one of these approaches uses revenue shares in their standardized structures, but instead deal exclusively in securities equity and debt. Why is that? Why, when in fact, all company value truly and inherently originates from revenues and profits earned from the original intellectual property?

Therefore, what is needed is an industry-wide, generally accepted legal structure that encapsulates certain clear parameters that those in the industry can understand and agree to.

What I am revealing above, is an artificially created dynamic that does not represent the truth, and yet this perspective decisively closes off other available options for inventors. The implications of this far exceed what initially meets the eye. It has led us collectively in a direction that does not serve us.

The entire financial industry and its regulatory agencies are primarily focused on high investor returns and protecting investors, while inventors are left to fend for themselves. An inventor can do well, assuming they know how to aggressively negotiate a good deal with their funders; however, their well-being is often much less of a priority in such a dynamic. This represents a real skew in our priorities, with disastrous long-term effects for us all.

A SECONDARY BURDEN ON THE BACKS OF INVENTORS: THE VENTURE CAPITAL MODEL ITSELF

K.I.S.S. represents the principle that most systems work best if they are kept simple rather than complicated. Therefore, simplicity is a key goal in any design with unnecessary complexity avoided.

Independent of one's view of the strengths and weaknesses of the venture capital (VC) model, one must point to the inherent and ubiquitous flaw of the VC structure itself. A respectable standard return expectation for any VC is 20% compound return. Specifically, VC fees include a 2% management fee annually, and a 20% share of the upside. Because the average VC performance expectation is that 8 of their 10 portfolio companies will ultimately flounder or fail, they really need 2 companies in their portfolio to perform as home runs. They are on a perpetual search for the ever evasive 'unicorns," which do happen of course, but not all that often.

Angel Blog and many other observers argue that when VC funds enter the scene, exit timeframes can often dramatically increase from 7-12 years. As more and more time goes on, more dilution naturally occurs for equity investors due to additional higher financing rounds. The pressure keeps building, as more money coming in means a higher exit price is necessary for respectable investor returns. It is not uncommon to hear that some VC's have from time to time blocked an earlier opportunity to sell if they cannot achieve their goal of 10-30x returns.

Why then is this dynamic added onto the back of an inventor who needs some simple startup capital? Inventors are, in effect, being forced to prove the viability of 2 business models, when only their own is needed. This is where the VC design represents a remarkable 'fly in the ointment." All these agendas are operating behind the scenes when an inventor may not ever want to sell their company, or may at least desire to be able to retain the right to make that choice. These inherent complications make things a bit twisted and messy regarding competing agendas and outcomes.

VC's need the Unicorns, and yet the Unicorns often do not like or want this cumbersome arrangement. So, Unicorns remain hard to find. The VC model at its core is counterintuitive and often works against its own success, and often, even against those it was designed to support.

THE COST TO US ALL ...

I have personally found that seriously significant disruptors are not interested in exits forced upon them by the VC model. They will particularly avoid working with them if they know they can truly disrupt an industry or two… or three, often waiting underground for the right situation to present itself, or the right heart that will honor their vision.

Sometimes, that person never comes. Sometimes these inventors and visionaries die with their inventions never seeing the light of day.

AND THAT IS A GREAT TRAGEDY FOR US ALL.

FINANCIAL INDUSTRY
DYNAMICS & CONSEQUENCES OVER TIME

STOCK MARKET
~ $30 Trillion

- Casino-like qualities
- Volatile
- Emotion-based
- Can destablize entire world economies quickly

VENTURE CAPITAL SECTOR
~ $5.7 TRILLION

M&A ~ $609 Billion
IPO ~ $3.9Trillion

- Loss of sovereignty
- Leads to monopoly-like dynamics
- Leads to unhealthy power dynamics

REVENUE SHARE SECTOR
N/A

- N/A because this does not exist as a current market sector, yet this is the truest representative of inherent value
- It is stable and represents a stabilizing effect.

SUMMARY

- The stock market has demonstrated repeated patterns of chaos and financial crises that can potentially drive the U.S. and world economies off the cliff because it is inherently unstable.
- The venture capital sector is a driver for the loss of inventor sovereignty. Over time this can lead to a loss of nation/state sovereignty, which in turn leads to too much power in the hands of a few.
- The SRTE® proposed model has the potential to bring about stable, long-term and peaceful global dynamics because it is based on inherent value represented by actual revenues.

DYNAMICS OVER TIME

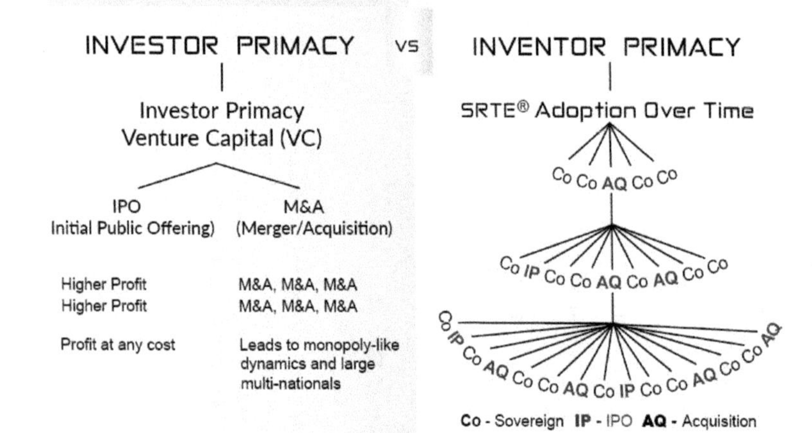

POTENTIAL CONSEQUENCES

- Prevents inventor/visionary free choice
- Incentivizes blind consumption
- Leads to centralized power
- Drives degradation of the natural world
- Causes global economic instability
- Creates oligopoly
- Promotes casino dynamics
- Results in volatility
- This dynamic creates an insatiable beast
- Although the market has it obvious benefits, its fault lies in its being a manipulated platform

- Supports local economic stability
- Creates local employment
- Leads to decentralized power
- Enables a return to U.S. national sovereignty
- Enables a return to national sovereignty for All Nations
- Supports more balanced international dynamics honoring local creation, inventions and unique cultural offerings from all nations
- Provides free choice/free will for creators, inventors and visionaries

Chapter 3

INVESTOR PRIMACY

THE DEEPER AND MORE INSIDIOUS ROOT of this entire dynamic however, is based on our historic focus exclusively on investor benefits, rather than inventor benefits as our primary priority. With this priority in place, high investor returns are designed to legally supersede the priority to support inventors and their innovations appropriately.

This perspective innately and inevitably corrupts human creativity, while undermining a company's integrity and welfare. The dominoes continue to fall. By consistently incentivizing the sale of one company to another through the VC/PE model and industry, we have very effectively corrupted our entire financial system at its core.

This seemingly innocuous and simple shift in our lens regarding our intentions and priorities almost exclusively towards the investor has inevitably led us in a direction that clearly does not serve us. Not individually, or collectively.

This tiny little seed has led to some very large implications. As these dynamics play out over time, it helps to create the inevitable result of monopoly-like dynamics. As relatively smaller companies must continually sell out and be swallowed up by the highest bidders again and again to continue to provide higher investor returns, where do we end up?

Understand that all public and private companies, and their board members have a legal, fiduciary responsibility to provide higher and higher returns to shareholders over time. It is their job in fact, before any other consideration, and beyond the consequences to the planet, employees, everything. This brilliantly short-sighted move was started in 1919, and it is called "shareholder primacy." Therefore, over time, inventors in all nation states are eventually forced to sell out their local, homegrown innovations to large multinationals, which leads to an imbalance of power and global financial instability, destroying many local economies in the process.

These multinationals must then also play by these same rules and are incentivized and motivated by beneficial tax dynamics or lower labor costs to achieve higher and higher shareholder returns. What the hell are we doing?! We consistently incentivize the monster of monopoly and global monoliths, and then wonder why it keeps happening.

WE KEEP FEEDING THE BEAST.

Chapter 4

THAT PESKY MONOPOLY ISSUE...

IT SEEMS TO ME that nobody really likes the idea of monopoly dynamics much, and yet we created a system that encourages almost exclusively that. Think about it. Given enough time, this becomes almost the exclusive outcome with the venture model that primarily feeds and incentivizes mergers and acquisitions.

The venture model is simple enough. Someone needs money. Someone gives them money. Again, the only way that investor can currently get a return using the structure of this particular model is for the inventor to sell out or go public.

Excluding the occasional IPO (initial public offering), this will lead to merger/acquisition after merger/acquisition after merger/acquisition to continually achieve consecutive investor returns on their investments. Every stage of a company's life where the

VC model is involved is dictated by this dynamic. It doesn't take a long time to figure out why each industry sector is currently dominated by the same 5-6 companies today. This gives us the illusion of choice due to different branding, but it's all the same, with the same owners and shareholders. We have in effect created our own nemesis. And the illusion is that we have free choice. Acquiring companies just keep getting bigger and bigger, as we continue down this predictable path towards the outcomes we are currently witnessing.

Even when a company does instead IPO rather than get acquired, the stock market then demands a higher and higher return to investors, and the beast remains insatiable. How far out of balance do we need to let this get? Is there a stopgap we can put in place at some point?

HINT: THE ANSWER IS YES, WHICH IS WHAT THIS BOOK IS ABOUT.

OK. Now, let's really put the nail in the coffin.

Again, if we consider legal precedence to ensure that this is the primary priority in this dynamic and consider it as almost a criminal act should someone dare to hold the intention to support an inventor as the priority rather than the investor, well, we have a problem. This dynamic becomes unseemly at a minimum, and highly destructive and dangerous in the context of power dynamics. Can you see this?

Oh, but we're not done yet. Let's then create an agency to enforce all of this. Wow, it's all tied up in a neat little package. But did anyone really think about the long-term implications of the cascade of these specific choices and actions?

Human society has known for centuries that too much power in a few hands is not a good thing, eloquently conveyed by the timeless proverb "absolute power absolutely corrupts."

Enough said.

SOME UNSOLICITED ADVICE

Should an inventor or company prefer to stay sovereign or keep their options open regarding a possible exit in the future, they would not be advised to use the fundraising VC model initially. If an inventor is committed to sell as soon as possible, the VC model offers a great modality to do so. It simply closes off other options in the process. That is an appropriate choice providing you are absolutely sure with no doubt in your mind regarding what path you want to take with your company and how you want to achieve that. No thing you could ever imagine could possibly transpire in the future that would cause you to make a different choice. In fact, you have explored every possible possibility that could ever present itself and your position remains the same. Fantastic! Go VC.

But if you are not sure……perhaps having another option would be a nice thing. After all things can change, and do, all the time. Beyond advice, an inventor may need some leverage to navigate this landscape.

Should you think I might be on to something here, let's do a simple internal inquiry regarding whether this may become well accepted. Ask yourself these questions, and then imagine how others might also respond:

- Do you believe in free will?
- Do you believe in free choice?
- Do you believe that you should have the right to change your mind?
- Do you think you have the right to choose your own destiny?
- Do you believe that an inventor is at least as important as an investor?
- Do you think we are honoring our creators now?
- Do you think our financial sector is serving our best interests?

Most importantly:

- Are you able to let go of the *MINDSET* that what we have now is the only way to do things?
- Are you ready to consider doing things differently?

These are important things to consider, because if we really want things to change, we have to be willing to *change*. Simply shifting things around in the old VC model or adding new regulation is not going to get us there. We need to change at a deeper level.

Chapter 5

HOW DID WE GET HERE?

AN INVENTOR'S OBSERVATION

"While I can appreciate venture capital (VC) support and know-how, they don't necessarily understand the soul of what I am doing or why I am doing it. Oftentimes, their only motivation is how much money they can make because of me and my idea, and how fast they can make it.

I get pushed out of the driver's seat and deemed incompetent to lead, but they are often leading it in the wrong direction. I understand that our values are different, ok, but why are their values deemed more important than mine?

And when did we all decide that money invested was more valuable than the actual idea it is supporting?"

AWARENESS

What is important to understand is that we cannot achieve the change that we want with the same systems in place, nor can we do it with the same level of awareness, or consciousness that created these systems.

It is often said that to change anything, we need to make the change within ourselves first before that change can be reflected outside of us in the material world. But how do we ACTUALLY DO THAT? We are the co-creators of our reality because we react to everything that happens to us in one way or another. So, to approach finance in a new way, there are some things we need to consider and become more aware of within ourselves first.

CHANGE!

There is much talk that we want to create a new world. Hallelujah!

However, if we want to really inspire the higher vibrational levels of human behavior such as trust or generosity, we need to create new structures that support and enable this to happen. It will behoove us to subsequently institutionalize these new systems over time should they make sense, just as we have with previous systems, but in a more conscious manner. If we do become clear that the new structures are aligned with the direction we want to go, institutional backing will better enable them to become more quickly adopted as the new standard for all. It will help to facilitate the turning of the tide. In the end, the people themselves can make the choice real-time to participate or not. Free will is critical in this transition. The truth of the more useful system will organically reveal itself over time. The tool presented in this book is only one small change. However, it represents a congruent choice, i.e., the energy is aligned, where the action supports the new intention, and the desired outcome is of less fear and greed, and more abundance and security for all.

There are technologies coming that will assist humanity to make some important evolutionary leaps. The truth of that will become self-evident over time. In the meantime, if we want to support these new technologies, we need to be financing them from a different level of consciousness, supported by financial tools that emanate from a higher consciousness to ensure their highest success. Do keep in mind that high profit is still the goal, as this actually represents a true reflection of a successful and beneficial company. But how we get there is different.

Congruence, congruence, congruence is the key.

THE INEXTRICABLE NATURE OF MONEY AND ENERGY, BUT AS RESONANCE!

Many have talked over recent years about the nature of money. How money is in effect "energy," and the importance of the fact that no energy should remain stagnant, as it leads inevitably to dysfunction and consequent illness. Whether it is exemplified in a pool of water or in the human spiritual, emotional or physical realms, this is a generally understood principle. But this is only engaging the topic on the superficial, basic level.

There is an entirely separate consideration that I would like to share with you. It is not simply whether money moves or stays put, but rather how it moves when it does. Specifically, the intention behind how money flows, has a particular resonance. Resonance impacts outcome. This is much more refined beyond whether money is simply moving or not. Therefore, becoming more aware of the energy 1 (emotion) behind the energy 2 (movement) is just as important as the movement itself, perhaps even more so. Quantum physicists understand this very clearly regarding the energy behind any action. The "field" directly impacts the material plane, and thus the reality we consequently experience. This includes the resonance within the field. Should you continue to remain unaware of the field you are part of creating and how it may impact your outcomes, you are really working with just half the deck towards generating any positive outcome.

David Hawkins, MD, PhD, while not a physicist, has also addressed this subject albeit in a different manner, and very simply in his book, Power vs Force, with his famed Map of Consciousness. Regardless of whether you agree with his methodology or not, he makes an inarguable fact. Anger, rage, and jealousy are not the same for us to be around as joy, bliss, and compassion. In other words, they resonate differently.

SPECIFIC INVESTOR EXAMPLE:

For example, are you aware of how you feel when you're actually making an investment? What if the driving energy around funding an inventor is about fear, pride, or greed? Think about it. If there is fear (fear of failure), if there is pride (it is not about supporting that inventor, but it is about you instead), and if there is greed (it is more about making as much money as possible, rather than ensuring the highest success of the company), do you think any of that represents congruent energy towards a positive outcome? If on the other hand, the intention is about love (love of the inventor and their technology and what it offers humanity) service (ensuring the inventors have all the support they need) and abundance, (making sure that the inventor has enough resources to fulfill the potential of their creation), these emotions give off a different resonance. Now we're headed in the right direction because these emotions and therefore your resonance are in congruent support of new creation.

As we contemplate the greater implications of this overall, we come to realize that we have created a financial industry which feeds and incentivizes greed, which is not particularly high on the continuum. This is not a judgement, but it is an observation. We have set up a system that incentivizes our lower resonance behavior patterns.

Well, how can we then blame, berate, and penalize each other from acting from this place or for learning to play this game well, when the "rules" have been set up this way?

We alone created this system.

WE created this game.

And then we institutionalized it.

INTENTION

There is another aspect of this dynamic that I mentioned above, beyond resonance. This is that one's specific intention behind something leads to a certain type of action that one takes in the 'material' plane, which then leads to a particular outcome. Different intentions lead to different outcomes.

Therefore, each time one changes one's intention, a shift is instigated that organically ripples through this internal dynamic of creation, which then becomes directly reflected in the material realm, i.e., our current reality.

EXAMPLE

If my intention is to stabilize a particular dynamic, such as war, I would work to enable peace. I would work towards dropping the reactivity of each side by trying to reveal the respective humanity in the other, as well as the pain they are in that may be causing a certain behavior. I would work to help others drop the emotional intensity and help them to step back with curiosity regarding the emotions they are feeling, to dive a little more deeply into where they themselves are coming from. Emotions may be directly related to the current situation of course, but surprisingly, they can often have nothing at all to do with what is happening right now. There is much information available within…it's like digging for gold within oneself. Lastly, I would work to increase the ability of a group of people to see the other group's humanity, beyond the individual lens. There is often collective trauma that has never been resolved from our collective or individual past history which is being acted out currently.

These considerations represent a short list of various approaches that one might use to diffuse a situation.

If on the other hand, I truly liked war or even profited from war, I would take the exact opposite actions based on my intentions. This would increase the likelihood of war which would achieve a very different outcome. Those actions would be to increase the angry rhetoric, amplify the differences and increase separation. I would increase the level of emotionality around the conflict, and work to increase the outrage and indignation of one group against another. I would work to reduce the perception of the other sides' humanity and reduce them to something lower than human, and therefore appropriate to eliminate.

Realize that neither of these intentions is incapable of being changed or reversed. These actions can be changed on either side, at any point in time, to enable very different outcomes. There is freedom and space in this awareness.

Awareness of this enables greater flexibility in this dynamic. That is why it is important to understand that nothing is in actuality, rigid, except perhaps our belief systems and our ideology.

Although these things can be difficult to change, they can indeed by changed. And this gives me great hope overall, regarding any number of subjects, but specifically regarding our ability to effect change for better outcomes.

Our Perspective impacts how we see reality.

Beyond the money, energy, resonance and action interplay, there is another piece of this puzzle to next consider.

Because if we don't see reality clearly, then how can we possibly fix our collective reality?

PERSPECTIVES AND HOW WE "SEE"

How we "see" and how we then *interpret* what we see has vast implications for the range of solutions we can bring to the table to rectify a problem.

For example, we all watch the same movie at a movie theater, and yet, we all have very different reactions to that film. Why is that? It's interesting when you think about it. It's the same film!

Different life experiences cause this divergence. Something that deeply triggers or touches one person because of their personal life experience, may not touch anything at all in another person who did not share that same experience. It is truly so helpful to understand that we all have different life experiences. Some things inspire creativity in some, where in others, the fear of the challenge causes them to contract instead. The point is, it is important to know that we all interpret differently, which leads to different courses of action.

This again implies there is some flexibility here by just knowing this. Nothing is really "fixed," least of all, any of our man-made systems.

Again, with a bit of personal self-reflection, you have likely already noticed yourself that there are certain ways that you look at things, which represent your different perspectives. What we "see and hear" is subsequently affected by a great deal of unconscious perspectives, which in turn colors everything we see and hear. How we interpret everything currently happening in our lives is based on our past, "already-lived" experiences, which then forms this unconscious yet powerful "lens" of interpretation. This interpretation then impacts the actions we decide to take today real-time, which leads to specific outcomes in our current lives. As we become more and more aware of this quiet dynamic, we become more empowered as individuals by becoming less unconsciously impacted by our past. Instead, in our present-day decision making, we are more able to observe and discern the current situation in a clear, unhindered manner, which leads to better decision making overall. An unobstructed view enables more clarity to be able to engage all aspects of the problem most effectively.

Therefore, if we see a real issue which is quietly underlying the finance industry itself, rather than wildly claiming capitalism is bad, or the world needs socialism as the only way to care for one another, then we are missing some real keys to finding useful and effective answers. This latter approach is highly effective in keeping us separated rather than enabling some excellent creative collaboration to take place. This again, is not in our collective interest.

I explain all of this because if we do not understand how our perspective impacts how we see reality, we become vulnerable to mistaking an "idea" for a "truth" which can lead to grave consequences.

MISTAKING AN IDEA FOR A TRUTH

We often act and behave as though all the structures and systems we have created are some kind of "immutable keystones" in the creation of civilized society. They are not. They can be changed, adapted, put to the side even if they no longer serve. Ideally, they can be somewhat retooled to better adapt to what is needed today, based on humanity's current place in our own evolutionary process. We can indeed be flexible. I'd like to elaborate a bit more here if I may.

The reason why it is important to understand how our perspective impacts how and what we see, is because this phenomenon occurs in a very significant and important way in relation to the Truth. Many understand when something occurs often enough or is repeated often enough, it can often be mistaken for the "Truth" and it is therefore unchangeable. Edward Bernays, who pioneered this methodology of propaganda and public relations, understood this phenomenon very well. Propaganda can hide a truth, or it can purport a truth. Either way, this becomes dangerous because we are not dealing with a clear view of the true situation.

If we "see" something as a truth, either personally or collectively, then it cannot be adjusted and it cannot be changed. If we do not "see" it that way, we can allow more openness and creativity around it. We can even throw it away if it doesn't serve us anymore.

However, real danger presents itself if a false "truth" is then subsequently institutionalized. It then becomes even more deeply enshrined into society and our societal norms, making it harder to put an end to it. When this occurs, it then graduates to the "gold standard" and becomes an incontrovertible methodology regarding how we do things. It also becomes invisible. This exact phenomenon has occurred within many industries, including our financial industry, leading to significant negative implications for all of us. I will share with you how this has specifically occurred in the next chapters.

But in conclusion, these examples demonstrate that how we "see," coupled with our "intentions," and the "resonance" of these intentions, along with our current mindsets regarding what can change and what cannot, what is truth and what is not, are critical to breaking through to a new solution. Each piece has significant implications for us as we forge a new course. These unconscious dynamics within ourselves keep us blocked as a collective, and more awareness of them can help set us free.

One path leads to being blaming or reproaching of others, while feeling stuck and frustrated. The other path leads to greater creativity, expansiveness, some fun and some real resolution.

With our eyes open, and more of us coming to understand this dynamic, we see that we can indeed engage more cards on the table. We become more empowered together to approach the world of finance in a new way, as well as any sector for that matter.

When we do, specifically in finance, as it is the silent keystone to so many other sectors, I believe the implications of this change will be breathtaking for us all.

Chapter 6

A NEW VISION:

REBALANCING INVENTORS AND INVESTORS BY HONORING THE CREATOR FIRST

IT IS A MOMENT...

Indeed, this is a moment of unprecedented crossroads in human history. Considering the many challenges concerning us all regarding population challenges, water scarcity, food scarcity and contamination, climate challenges, terrorism, and war, we are presented with endless opportunities for new solutions and a new vision from brilliant new thinkers.

Therefore, we need all hands-on deck to bring all of humanity's intelligence and creativity to bear.

WHAT A NEW PERSPECTIVE DOES

What if, as we engage these challenges, we were to gently shift our priorities just a little while we were doing so… just a smidge… what could that mean, if anything, to our current global dynamics? Not much? Or everything?

For example, what if we did indeed change "Investor Primacy" to "Inventor Primacy?" What would that mean to us? Just one little letter change. Would our world change as a result?

NOVELTY OF A NEW APPROACH

A new financial approach has been created that represents a subtle yet deeply significant paradigm shift regarding our priorities surrounding creation.

It was conceived from an entirely different perspective and value system regarding how entrepreneurial funding and innovation can be achieved. This new lens delivers a different type of solution with significant long-term implications that will realign and support our creators to quickly bring forth the solutions this planet and all life on it so critically needs.

This different intention leads to different actions that will lead to different outcomes for all stakeholders. It will enable these stakeholders to mutually benefit in a new standardized way, while propelling the entire creation and entrepreneurial world into a whole new paradigm.

Over time, the implementation of this model as an alternative to the VC model can lead to greater global security and more balanced power dynamics between all parties, from the micro (inventor/investor, company), macro (national) and meta (global) perspectives, with significant implications for global economic stability.

Quantum law clearly demonstrates through the works of some key quantum physicists such as Young or Piccaluga that intention and conscious awareness dramatically impact the outcomes of any said endeavor or creation. I mentioned this earlier with David Hawking's work, as well as the ontological coaching references in the first chapter, but suffice it to say that there is a multi-disciplined consensus that is growing worldwide, arriving at the conclusion that the truth of this relationship, or invisible dynamic, exists and is becoming evident to all. Put another way, it has entered the collective zeitgeist so to speak. I am simply helping it land specifically within the financial realm.

This model was created from an intention to honor and respect our visionaries and inventors as its priority. Coupled with its private blockchain to ensure greater trust and transparency for all stakeholders if desired, it is offered as a powerful foundational component towards this end, while honoring quantum principals at its core. This option incentivizes diversity, competition, and decentralized power.

Because of the integral blockchain aspect of this approach, it may also easily fit into some new, future financial systems or structures that others may create. Its introduction will specifically address the entrepreneurial puzzle piece to this broader new financial puzzle.

As I mentioned, there are truly profound new technologies that will be coming available to us and how we will fund these new technologies becomes critically important. The intention of our funding needs to be truly aligned through similar values and similar resonance. The unintended lack of awareness of the resonances of scarcity, fear and greed reflected in our current financial systems can simply no longer interfere with these higher-level inventions. Those values corrupt the "field," and hinder our odds for success. Therefore, it would not behoove us to continue to institutionalize them in our financial sector.

"THE DOGMAS OF THE QUIET PAST ARE INADEQUATE TO THE STORMY PRESENT. THE OCCASION IS PILED HIGH WITH DIFFICULTY, AND WE MUST RISE WITH THE OCCASION. AS OUR CASE IS NEW, SO WE MUST THINK ANEW, AND ACT ANEW."

-PRESIDENT ABRAHAM LINCOLN,
DECEMBER 1, 1862,
AT HIS SECOND STATE OF
THE UNION ADDRESS

Chapter 7

THE SOVEREIGN REVENUE TRUST ENTITY OR SRTE®

THE SOON TO BE LAUNCHED Sovereign Revenue Trust Entity® or SRTE® represents a new patent-pending application in the entrepreneurial domain of the financial industry. It will represent a real alternative to Venture Capital and Private Equity (PE) funding, while honoring and serving inventors and visionaries as its *priority*.

The SRTE® enables scenarios that cannot easily happen in the current financial industry. Pooled outside investors, as well as VC's, PE's etc. are now offered the standardized ability to invest and share in the revenue streams of private companies they would simply have no access to otherwise. Although this first book discusses primarily the vision that underlies a potential solution, a second book is forthcoming that will address the actual model itself.

THE SRTE® IN A NUTSHELL

- The Sovereign Revenue Trust Entity® or SRTE® platform represents a viable, patent-pending alternative to the venture capital (VC) model for inventors and entrepreneurs.
- The SRTE® is a standardized new investment structure tied to its own privately integrated blockchain.
- The SRTE® enables a new way to raise capital to establish initial ownership through a fungible entity which enables various choices versus a forced exit.
- The SRTE® prevents the forced sale of a smaller company to a larger acquirer that is demanded by, and integral to the VC/PE model.
- It protects inventors as a priority, effectively ending the 'pillaging' of our creators that often occurs. The SRTE® does not alienate VC's or PE's but rather enhances their potential offerings to their investors.
- The SRTE® rebalances the inventor-investor dynamic from "top-to-bottom" with often competing agendas to a balanced "side-by-side" dynamic, thereby ensuring shared and mutual agendas that will logically enhance the odds of entrepreneurial success.

- The SRTE® enables and supports innovation and employment to stay local or national, serving the interests of national sovereignty, while diffusing the continual creation of large multinationals.
- The SRTE® model honors Creation at its core, representing a paradigm shift in the financial sector regarding how we support our innovators.

Venture capital firms, private equity funds, and corporations will also be able to share in this new opportunity, while startup companies will gain much greater scalability more efficiently, with no risk to their IP or control of their companies.

The SRTE® is designed with inventors as its first priority. Inventors should not be forced to sell their company or IP (intellectual property) to gain initial funding, or mezzanine level funding to enable growth, as they are in the VC model. The SRTE® prevents a forced exit strategy that is demanded in the VC scenario.

The SRTE® ensures that an inventor's IP and company sovereignty are always protected. It also ensures that outside interests will no longer dictate the terms of how an inventor's technology is engaged, solely from the perspective of highest profits at the expense of all other considerations.

The SRTE® structure is useful for any Inventor that desires to raise funds to launch a new company, restructure a current company's investors or ownership, reduce dilution, or for mezzanine financing. It will prove exceptionally useful for any company, yet especially for truly innovative, industry disruptive technologies, as these have the significant potential to become billion-dollar valuations due to their highly disruptive nature. As such, these inventors may often choose to remain private and not be subjected to manipulation by outside interests regarding the intent of the use of their technologies.

VARIOUS SRTE® SCENARIOS

- A parent company can engage the SRTE® to find partners, strategic supporters, or funding.
- PE's, VC's, or broker/dealers may license the SRTE® model to fund a parent company.
- A parent company can license the SRTE® to regain control of the company itself, to mitigate or even reverse dilution.
- Financial incubators may license the SRTE® to fund startup companies.
- Later stage scenarios such as mezzanine and growth capital instruments may license the SRTE®.
- A corporation may license the right to use

the SRTE® to gain access to revolutionary private technologies that complement their current product portfolios.

- An inventor/parent company may theoretically decide to engage with two SRTE® licenses. The first being a free-standing SRTE®, and the other occurs through a separate VC who licenses the right to use the SRTE® to bring the resources of their current investor base to bear. In this way, the parent company can access two different investor bases simultaneously, while offering current VC investors an opportunity to participate in the portfolio companies' revenues they would never have access to under their current circumstances.

Chapter 8

PEACE, INDUSTRY TRANSITION AND FOUNDER'S SYNDROME

A NATURAL SYMBIOSIS

"BLESSED ARE THE PEACEMAKERS, FOR THEY WILL BE CALLED THE CHILDREN OF GOD."

Human beings are messy. We just are.

It kind of comes with the turf, I'm afraid.

For instance, there is a dynamic called "Founder's Syndrome" in startups and companies in any stage of development. This "syndrome" is a serious and tremendous challenge that can take a company down. Many in the VC world often dismiss founders or inventors as inappropriate business leaders. The Sagesse Platform does not share this view; however, a means does need to be created to enable business leaders to work together effectively with brilliant, often "mad scientist" creators, while also being responsible and pragmatic regarding the use of investment funds to build a company.

The delicate matter of ascertaining each player's strengths, weaknesses, and knowhow, particularly regarding the inventors, founders and advisors is crucial to understand from the beginning.

An ideal situation might look something like this:

Each player in the startup scenario needs to have or develop the capacity to self-reflect and acknowledge things about themselves that are generally self- evident to everyone else, excluding of course, the individual themselves. By the way, a little humor along the way is most helpful. Each player needs to better develop the skill of observation without judgement, so the team can feel comfortable reflecting uncomfortable things to one another from the place of shared goal and intention, rather than a personal attack or judgement. One critical thing to know is that we all screw up. That's a good place to start, and no one is immune.

A means of resolving and transmuting conflict needs to be agreed upon amongst all parties, so that when the inevitable challenge arises, there is a roadmap available to all to enable a way through it. Rather than engaging the board of directors to exclusively play that role, the Sagesse Platform prefers engaging a team of coaches and skilled conflict transformation experts who have helped to successfully rebuild and reconnect societies and communities torn apart by genocide, or extreme mutual violence. Individuals with this level of capacity will be very skilled at helping businesspeople resolve different opinions and ideas about the direction of the company. If hearts can be reconnected with the magnitude of challenges in the former scenario, they can surely be successful in connecting hearts in the latter scenario.

The Sagesse Platform has cultivated an extensive network with many peace builders, coaches, and mediation professionals in the field of conflict transformation all over the world. Their strengths are often in the areas considered "soft," in that they represent a reconnection of the human hearts on either side of a conflict or opposing view. But these "soft" differences can and do annihilate companies, and represent a powerful source of destruction within many relationships, whether they be personal, business or in relationships between nations.

The skillsets of these coaching and peace building networks can offer crucial support for new teams impassioned by what they are bringing to the table for us all. These special people are highly skilled at building personal competency to be able to step outside of the "self," to connect more deeply within oneself and with others, and to reveal underlying unconscious agendas that can silently disrupt the best laid plans of many companies. I just mentioned above that these skills are often referred to as "soft," but I beg to differ. I have found that this is the hardest and deepest work to engage with, as human hearts and minds are complicated. And emotional. What's worse, we are not remotely educated in these arenas in most of our educational backgrounds. Crazy! These realms need a delicate, skilled, and sensitive touch if companies are to become successful and then stay successful. Ideally, many will learn how to ride the wild waves and troughs of entrepreneurship individually and together, to reduce the incidence of so many failed companies. If we do this together, we stand a much better chance of building stronger camaraderie, intimacy, and synergy among team players, increasing the likelihood of stronger and more stable companies. I don't know about you, but a 70-80% failure rate of most VC portfolios does not represent a successful model to me. Something is missing. And it's clearly not about ownership, as the success rate should reflect that. It does not.

Transitions within industries themselves that are experiencing a critical leapfrog dynamic need to be negotiated carefully and thoughtfully, to mitigate the negative collateral damage often associated with and feared by those of the old system. Easing the transition for those currently employed for example, while capitalizing on their industry knowledge so that an inventor does not have to start from scratch regarding networks, infrastructure, knowhow, etc. will save tremendous time as we co-create this new world together.

Chapter 9

STAKEHOLDER BENEFITS

INVENTORS

- The Creator is the Priority.
- No Forced Exits.
- Enables a choice over time regarding an exit strategy or remaining private.
- Rebalances power dynamics between funders and inventors.
- Maintains inventor sovereignty.
- No competitive internal agenda between VC funders and the inventor.
- One entity deals with a pool of investors under a different dynamic.
- The SRTE® adds additional leverage in your dynamics with VC funds.
- Reduces dilution with the potential to reclaim

ownership with the SRTE®.

- No risk of losing your IP when partnering with corporations for faster scalability.
- Option for private SRTE® blockchain to increase transparency for all partners.
- Side-by-side relationship rather than top-down relationship with your investors with the SRTE® represents a secondary revenue stream to current funds.
- The WBENC certification of Sagesse Holdings, parent company of Sagesse, LLC provides crucial advantages to new inventors by leveraging WBENC Public Relations power to create important corporate transparency and accountability when engaging with new start-ups.

INVESTORS

- Possibly faster liquidity dynamics rather than waiting for an exit.
- Possibly higher returns over the long term.
- Potentially shorter time frames for returns.
- Option for private SRTE® blockchain to increase transparency for all investors.
- Resolves the concern of dilution from subsequent financing rounds.
- Ability to participate in ending the bigger

scourge of monopoly, or certainly reducing the likelihood of creation of exceptionally large multinationals.

VENTURE CAPITAL | PRIVATE EQUITY FUNDS

- Access to private technology you normally could not access without the SRTE®.
- Licensing with the SRTE® represents the potential for an entirely new revenue stream for your investors.
- Licensing with the SRTE® enables a more diversified range of time frames, liquidity and returns to your investor base.
- Licensing with the SRTE® will reduce the intense pressure to find the home runs for investor returns.
- Rather than the race for an exit, a VC can instead support companies becoming strong over the long haul.
- Non-competing agendas will potentially increase the likelihood of creating more successful companies when all energy is focused in the same direction rather than diffused.

PENSION FUNDS | FAMILY OFFICES

- The SRTE® supports local innovation, therefore supporting strong local economies and employment. This in turn leads to more investment in your pension funds by keeping employees local.
- Strong employment leads to more pensioners. More strong local economies lead to more employment, directly enabling you to invest in your own future viability as a pension fund.
- Be a part of ending some monopoly-like dynamics through encouraged M & A's.
- Possibly faster liquidity dynamics for your investors rather than waiting for liquidity events.
- Possible higher returns by supporting strong growth resulting in strong revenue share.
- Will be able to support innovators while supporting the bigger vision of balancing power dynamics for our creators, honoring creators as our priority while supporting the effort to end the continual creation of large multi-nationals while stabilizing nations, and international economies.
- Will be part of supporting a vision for financing a new entrepreneurial platform that supports all stakeholders, in the interest of life on this planet.

- Will be a part of realigning the financial industry in service of Creation and human creativity.
- Be a part of actively changing our value systems on the planet, with the potential of entirely new outcomes.

CORPORATIONS

- Will gain access to technologies you simply would have no access to otherwise.
- The SRTE® enables more inventors to negotiate with greater leverage, which means more access for you.
- Will be able to reallocate resources to provide or retool current infrastructure for cutting edge innovation, leading to more direct revenue generation rather than expensive R&D.
- Reduces capital costs to transition industries with more players at the table in a balanced manner.
- Will be able to expand your product line by gaining access to innovations that could dramatically increase the efficacy of your own products and technology.
- The WBENC certification of Sagesse Holdings, parent company of Sagesse, LLC, provides excellent tax advantages, as well as positive PR for corporations.

GOVERNMENTS AND NATIONS

- The SRTE® supports national strength, economic viability, and sovereignty.
- The SRTE® supports local employment and innovation.
- The SRTE® destroys the seeds of monopoly, specifically to change the dynamic and consequences of M&A's (Mergers and Acquisitions).
- Nations may share in the revenues from each other's innovations, with no concern of loss of sovereignty for either or any nation.
- The SRTE® supports global economic stability, which is needed for growth in all sectors in all nations.
- The SRTE® honors local innovations, which are birthed from all cultures globally without denigrating the original creation or its creator by forcing that innovation into globalist structures.
- The SRTE® respects the diversity, beauty, and integrity of all human creation.

OUR NATURAL WORLD

- The SRTE® provides a tool to help our lawmakers in Congress to rebalance our behaviors and reduce the abuse of our natural world.

- By starting from a different value system of more balanced relationships, the SRTE® can mitigate the often-unchecked greed which has had such detrimental effects on our natural environment.
- There is balance in all systems that are stable, and the SRTE® can help return this balance to the entrepreneurial sector.
- "Blessed are the meek, for they shall inherit the Earth". The SRTE® helps return us to such timeless intentions, to the benefit of ourselves, our natural bio-systems, and all life.
- The SRTE® respects the creator, the Creator and all of creation itself. This is a consistent theme throughout all spiritual traditions, and it is this premise from which the SRTE® is conceived and birthed.
- The SRTE® honors the true quantum nature of our reality where everything is interconnected. As we strive to live in greater harmony with the natural world that supports all life, it would behoove us to reconsider our priorities. We will need a new tool to assist us to do that, and the SRTE® is one such offering.

Chapter 10

SOME ADDITIONAL TEETH

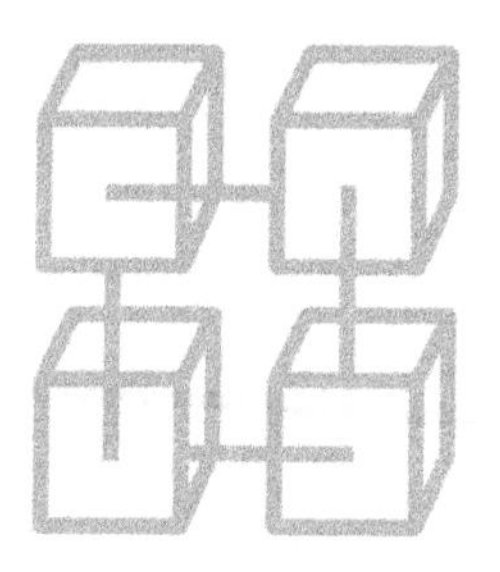

BLOCKCHAIN TECHNOLOGY

The SRTE® will include an option for inventors and visionaries if they like, to use its own safe and secure private blockchain platform. This will ensure end to end protection and complete transparency regarding a company's performance, and all agreements between parties as a means of ensuring honorability regarding commitments, agreements, fees and profit share distribution amongst all stakeholders to ensure transparency for all.

LEGAL REPRESENTATION

The largest law firm in the world, Dentons, LLC represents Sagesse, LLC as our patent attorneys and corporate law attorneys, located in New York City. Joel Bock, a partner and patent attorney at Dentons, is also a partner on the patent-pending new platform and methodology, the SRTE®. Trademarks are registered in the U.S. Patent and Trademark Office.

WBENC CERTIFICATION

The SRTE® inventor is a certified business owner with WBENC.

The Women's Business Enterprise National Council (WBENC), is the largest third-party certifier of businesses owned, controlled, and operated by women in the United States. WBENC is a national 501(c)(3) non-profit, and partners with 14 Regional Partner Organizations to provide its world class standard of certification to women-owned businesses throughout the country. WBENC fosters strong collaborations between women business owners and its extensive list of committed corporate partners.

As a Certified WBENC, Sagesse Holdings, LLC is in a unique position to capitalize on long term relationships nurtured for over 20 years between WBENC and its corporate partners interested in supporting women business owners. Although the current model was primarily created to incentivize providing contracts for women with these corporate partners, the SRTE®

model was created to complement and expand these dynamics between these two parties, offering significant benefits to WBENC itself.

The SRTE® Platform enhances the dynamic for WBENC certified businesses to become even more respected as peers with corporations, rather than acting exclusively as contractors employed by them. The ability for a corporation to expand its product portfolio while gaining greater economic efficiencies or revenues thanks to the business savvy and key relationships of a WBENC business owner, frankly, commands a different level of dynamic and respect.

Chapter 11

LAST REFLECTIONS

UNSOLICITED ADVICE

Do not let your lack of knowledge in a particular area preclude you from trying to fix a problem. I often times felt like an outsider in my career regarding the fact that I hadn't drilled down in one area of expertise or another, as so many others had chosen to do. However, over the years I realized that I typically observed structures from above and afar, from a rather unique perspective. My perceived "weakness" was actually my biggest strength. For example, I had never considered the finance industry or venture capital as an area of personal interest. Rather, it was a means to an end to support a healthcare technology that I believed the world needed years ago. However, it is because of my unplanned venture capital exposure that I was able to approach this whole scenario from a very practical, objective and frankly non-attached perspective. As such, it has enabled me to be able to see some things over time, and in different ways, that may not be evident to others. It's the whole "can't see the forest for the trees" phenomenon in action.

From not knowing "everything" about finance, I could instead be more creative as I wasn't attached to the current constructs. Rather than unconsciously being closed off from new thinking from being inculcated for years with 'THE" way to do things, I could more easily step out of standard thinking and create something new. I could see the flaws and the holes in the structures we created and consequently could be more creative in addressing the challenge these flaws inherently caused.

I am not alone in this. A colleague recently called me a "systems buster" just as she is herself. I had not been referred to in such a manner before, but it resonated for me. I think there are a lot more of us out there, even if we don't realize it yet. If we would simply *allow* ourselves to *give* ourselves the permission to let go of our current way of doing things, wow, we can release our own shackles! This to me represents the tremendous untapped potential of humanity that I am so excited about! I really hope this book inspires others to do the same in their respective industries and sectors. We could be having so much more fun than we currently are, freely co-creating together rather than a contraction and repression of ourselves though increased rules and regulation.

Many of us that can break free of the "social constructs" will play key roles in freeing us to do what we each truly came to do. I see a world where we become truly free on Earth to express and bring forth our unique and respective gifts to others. I have had this vision for years.

While blame and demonization represent the antithesis of all this, the truth is that neither of these approaches really fixes anything. We have all played our parts in this, so let's just own it, let it go, and move forward.

K.I.S.S.

Quantum physicist Pierre Piccaluga has often told me "les solutions les plus puissantes sont simples, pas complexes." "Simplicity is profoundly more powerful than complexity." He especially emphasizes "unnecessary complexity." This premise has certainly proven true in my own journey to create a new approach for the financial industry to help him and others.

Once one spends just a little time to understand what this model unveils through its simplicity, the brilliance of it begins to reveal itself. To be clear, I am not referring to any brilliance of mine, but rather the dynamic itself that is simply unveiled by the presence of this entity, and what it does to transform the financial landscape. Again, this was downloaded to me…in other words, it came as an inspiration. It did not come from my linear mind per se. I am clear that inspiration comes from the Creator, and that I am simply the shepard. I leave you with this, my humble attempt at eloquence, to convey what is in my heart. Although I am clear that I am no poet, I hope that you can nevertheless feel my intention.

THE SAGESSE OF CREATION

THERE IS THE SACREDNESS OF CREATION...
that must be honored with reverence and respect.
Manifested through the expression of...
all Life on this planet,
all Creation on this planet,
through Inventors and Visionaries who bring these
new creations through
the vessels of their hearts,
minds,
and souls...

When one looks at the cosmos and is awed
and moved by its exquisite beauty,
one understands that there exists a Divine order
that was not created to be destroyed, exploited,

or profited from, but to be revered, treasured,
and engaged through mutual respect.
Current models do not honor sacred creation
as its priority.
They are models of a different intent,
and they do have their place.

For those inventors and investors who are interested in simply selling their company as fast as possible, for as much money as possible, those models work brilliantly, and there is a multi-hundred-billion-dollar market sector that confirms this necessary dynamic.

However, there are also so many inventors in search of something else. Inventors who long to bring forth something more, in service to the beauty of life on this planet and our shared humanity. Inventors who want to build something of their own from their hearts that lasts, and for these inventors, another option is needed.

From this intention, the Sovereign Revenue Trust Entity® or SRTE® was inspired and created.

Barbara Guth

ABOUT THE AUTHOR

BARBARA GUTH is the Founder and CEO of Sagesse Holdings, LLC. In addition to funding, founding, and co-founding several startup companies, she was also a 9/11 first responder and has served on several-boards ranging from peacebuilding to high technology. Barbara has committed the last 21 years to searching the globe for the key technologies that could transform multiple sectors simultaneously, while assisting humanities' shift into the enlightened age. Barbara is honored to have established extensive global networks in the energy, healthcare, technology, finance, and peacebuilding/conflict transformation fields, who support her commitment to solve seemingly intractable global challenges with pragmatic, innovative solutions.

CPSIA information can be obtained
at www.ICGtesting.com
Printed in the USA
LVHW051942160523
747154LV00017B/870